REPUBLIC OF
CAPE VERDE

EST.
JULY 5, 1975

CAPE VERDE

Cabo Verde, also known as Cape Verde, is an archipelago located off the coast of West Africa. The islands were uninhabited until the 15th century when they were discovered by Portuguese explorers. The Portuguese quickly established settlements on the islands, using them as a base for the transatlantic slave trade.

Throughout the 16th and 17th centuries, Cabo Verde became an important hub for the slave trade, with thousands of Africans passing through the islands on their way to the Americas. The islands also served as a stopping point for ships traveling between Europe, Africa, and the Americas.

In the 19th century, Cabo Verde began to see a decline in its importance as a trading post, as the transatlantic slave trade was abolished and new shipping routes were established. The islands struggled economically, and many of its residents emigrated to other countries in search of better opportunities.

CAPE VERDE

In 1951, Cabo Verde was made an overseas province of Portugal, giving it limited self-governing powers. However, dissatisfaction with Portuguese rule continued to grow, and in 1975, following the Carnation Revolution in Portugal, Cabo Verde was granted independence.

Since gaining independence, Cabo Verde has made significant progress in developing its economy and improving the standard of living for its citizens. The country has a stable democratic government and has become a popular tourist destination, known for its beautiful beaches and vibrant culture.

Today, Cabo Verde is a member of several international organizations, including the United Nations and the African Union. The country continues to face challenges, including high levels of poverty and unemployment, but it remains a proud and independent nation with a rich history and culture.

CAPE VERDE

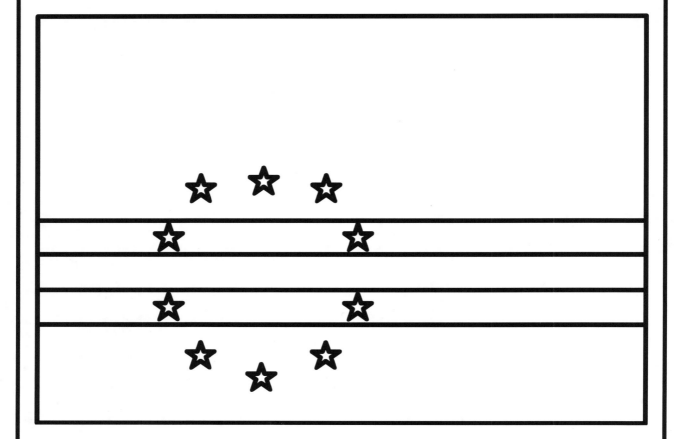

FLAG

FLAG HISTORY

The flag of Cape Verde was officially adopted on September 22, 1992, following the country's independence from Portugal in 1975. The flag features a horizontal band of blue at the top, a horizontal band of white in the middle, and a horizontal band of red at the bottom. In the center of the flag is a circle made up of ten yellow five-pointed stars, which represent the ten main islands of Cape Verde.

The colors of the flag have symbolic meanings: blue represents the sky and the ocean that surrounds the islands, white symbolizes peace, and red represents the struggle for independence. The yellow stars represent the unity of the islands and the hope for a bright future.

Before the current flag was adopted, Cape Verde used a flag that was similar to the current one but featured a different arrangement of colors and stars. The previous flag was used from 1975 to 1992, when it was replaced with the current design.

Overall, the flag of Cape Verde is a symbol of the country's history, culture, and aspirations for the future. It is a powerful representation of the unity and diversity of the Cape Verdean people and their connection to the land and sea that surrounds them.

NATIONAL FLOWER

GERBERA DAISY

NATIONAL FLOWER HISTORY

The Gerbera Daisy, also known as the African Daisy, is not only the national flower of Cape Verde, but it is also a popular flower worldwide. It is native to South Africa and was named after the German botanist Traugott Gerber.

The Gerbera Daisy has a long history of cultivation and has been grown for centuries for its vibrant colors and long-lasting blooms. It was first introduced to Europe in the 19th century and quickly became a favorite among gardeners and florists.

In Cape Verde, the Gerbera Daisy is prized for its beauty and symbolizes the country's natural beauty and diversity. It is often used in floral arrangements for special occasions and celebrations.

The Gerbera Daisy's popularity as a cut flower has led to the development of many different varieties, with a wide range of colors and sizes available. It is known for its bright, cheerful blooms and is often used to convey messages of happiness, joy, and friendship.

Overall, the Gerbera Daisy is a beloved flower in Cape Verde and around the world, cherished for its beauty and symbolism.

NATIONAL BIRD

GREY-HEADED KINGFISHER

NATIONAL BIRD HISTORY

The Grey-headed kingfisher (Halcyon leucocephala), also known as the Cape Verde kingfisher, is a species of bird that is native to Cape Verde, an archipelago off the coast of West Africa. The Grey-headed kingfisher is the national bird of Cape Verde and holds special significance in the country's culture and history.

The Grey-headed kingfisher is a small bird with a distinctive grey head, blue-green wings, and a bright orange belly. It is known for its striking appearance and melodious call, which has made it a popular symbol of beauty and grace in Cape Verdean folklore.

In Cape Verdean culture, the Grey-headed kingfisher is often associated with good luck and prosperity. It is believed that seeing a Grey-headed kingfisher is a sign of good fortune and blessings from the gods. The bird is also seen as a symbol of peace and harmony, as its presence is said to bring calm and tranquility to those who encounter it.

The Grey-headed kingfisher's status as the national bird of Cape Verde reflects the country's commitment to preserving its natural heritage and biodiversity. The bird serves as a symbol of Cape Verde's unique wildlife and the importance of conservation efforts to protect its natural habitats.

Overall, the Grey-headed kingfisher plays an important role in Cape Verdean culture and history, serving as a symbol of beauty, luck, and the country's rich natural heritage. Its presence in the country's landscape is a reminder of the importance of preserving and protecting the diverse wildlife that calls Cape Verde home.

HISTORICAL MONUMENTS

1. Cidade Velha (Old Town) – The first European settlement in the tropics, Cidade Velha is a UNESCO World Heritage Site and home to several historical monuments including the Royal Fortress of São Filipe and the Church of Nossa Senhora do Rosário.

2. Forte Real de São Filipe – Located in Cidade Velha, this fortress was built in the 16th century to protect the town from pirate attacks.

3. Pelourinho de Ribeira Grande – This pillory, located in the town of Ribeira Grande, was used during the colonial period for public punishments.

4. Forte de São João Baptista – Located in the town of Tarrafal on the island of Santiago, this fort was built in the 18th century to protect the town from pirate attacks.

5. Ponta do Sol Lighthouse – Built in 1896, this lighthouse is located in the town of Ponta do Sol on the island of Santo Antão.

HISTORICAL MONUMENTS

6. São Pedro Cathedral – Located in the capital city of Praia on the island of Santiago, this cathedral was built in the 19th century and is the seat of the Roman Catholic Diocese of Santiago de Cabo Verde.

7. Praça Alexandre Albuquerque – This historic square in Praia is home to several colonial-era buildings and monuments.

8. Igreja de Nossa Senhora do Rosário – Located in Cidade Velha, this church was built in the 15th century and is one of the oldest churches in Cape Verde.

9. Cemitério de Povoação Velha – This historic cemetery, located in the town of Povoação Velha on the island of Boa Vista, is home to several tombstones dating back to the 18th century.

10. Palácio do Povo – Located in Praia, this historic building was once the seat of government for Cape Verde and now houses the National Assembly.

BOA VISTA ISLAND

BOA VISTA ISLAND

Boa Vista is one of the ten islands that make up the Cape Verde archipelago, located off the coast of West Africa. The island was first discovered by Portuguese explorers in the 15th century and was initially uninhabited. It was later settled by Portuguese colonists and African slaves brought to the island to work on sugar plantations.

The island's main town, Sal Rei, was established as a port for the slave trade and later became a center for salt mining and fishing. Over the years, Boa Vista has also become a popular tourist destination, known for its beautiful beaches and clear waters.

Boa Vista is divided into two municipalities: Rabil and Boa Vista. Rabil is the smaller of the two municipalities and is located in the interior of the island, while Boa Vista is the larger municipality and is located along the coast.

In 1975, Cape Verde gained independence from Portugal and Boa Vista became a part of the newly formed republic. Since then, the island has continued to develop as a tourist destination, attracting visitors from around the world with its stunning landscapes and warm climate.

Today, Boa Vista is known for its laid-back atmosphere, friendly locals, and diverse cultural heritage. It remains an important part of Cape Verde's history and economy, contributing to the country's growing tourism industry.

BRAVA ISLAND

BRAVA ISLAND

Brava is a small island located in the southern part of Cape Verde, off the coast of West Africa. It is known for its rugged terrain, lush vegetation, and beautiful beaches. The island has a population of around 6,000 people and is one of the least populated islands in Cape Verde.

Brava was first inhabited by the Portuguese in the 16th century, who used the island as a base for slave trading. The island was later colonized by the Portuguese and became a center for agriculture, particularly coffee and sugarcane production.

The major municipalities on the island of Brava are Nova Sintra, the capital and largest city, Furna, and Nossa Senhora do Monte. Nova Sintra is the administrative and cultural center of the island, while Furna is known for its beautiful beaches and Nossa Senhora do Monte is a small village located in the mountains.

Brava became a part of Cape Verde in the 15th century when the Portuguese first discovered the islands. The island remained under Portuguese control until Cape Verde gained independence in 1975. Since then, Brava has been a part of the Republic of Cape Verde and is known for its unique culture, music, and cuisine.

Today, Brava is a popular destination for tourists looking to experience the natural beauty and tranquility of Cape Verde. The island is also known for its vibrant music scene, with traditional genres such as morna and coladeira being popular among locals and visitors alike.

FOGO ISLAND

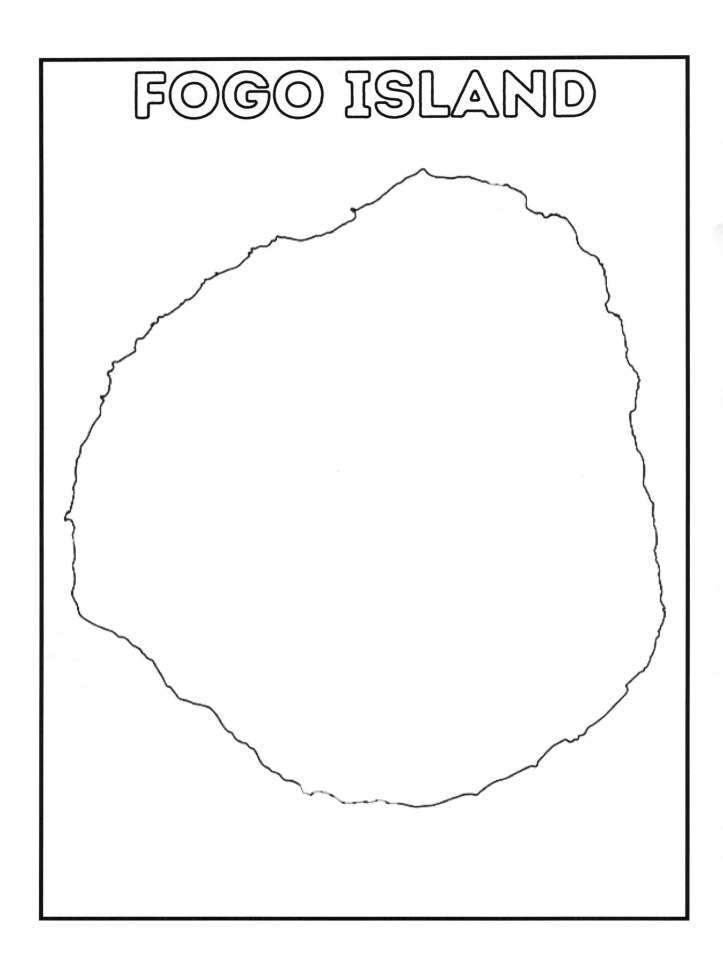

FOGO ISLAND

Fogo is an island in the Cape Verde archipelago, located in the central part of the Atlantic Ocean. The island is known for its active volcano, Pico do Fogo, which is the highest point in Cape Verde.

The island of Fogo has a long history, with evidence of human settlement dating back to the 15th century. The first recorded European contact with the island was in 1456, when Portuguese explorers arrived on the island. The Portuguese established a settlement on Fogo, which grew over the years into several major municipalities.

The major municipalities on the island of Fogo include São Filipe, Mosteiros, and Santa Catarina. São Filipe is the largest municipality on the island and serves as the capital of Fogo. Mosteiros is located on the western coast of the island and is known for its beautiful beaches and natural scenery. Santa Catarina is located on the eastern coast of the island and is known for its agricultural production.

Fogo became a part of Cape Verde in the 15th century, when the Portuguese colonized the archipelago. The island played a significant role in the transatlantic slave trade, serving as a stopover point for ships traveling between Africa and the Americas. In the 19th century, Fogo experienced a period of economic growth, with the establishment of coffee plantations on the island.

Today, Fogo is known for its unique landscape, with the active volcano Pico do Fogo attracting tourists from around the world. The island is also known for its rich cultural heritage, with a unique blend of Portuguese and African influences. Fogo is a popular destination for hikers and nature lovers, with its rugged terrain and stunning views.

MAIO ISLAND

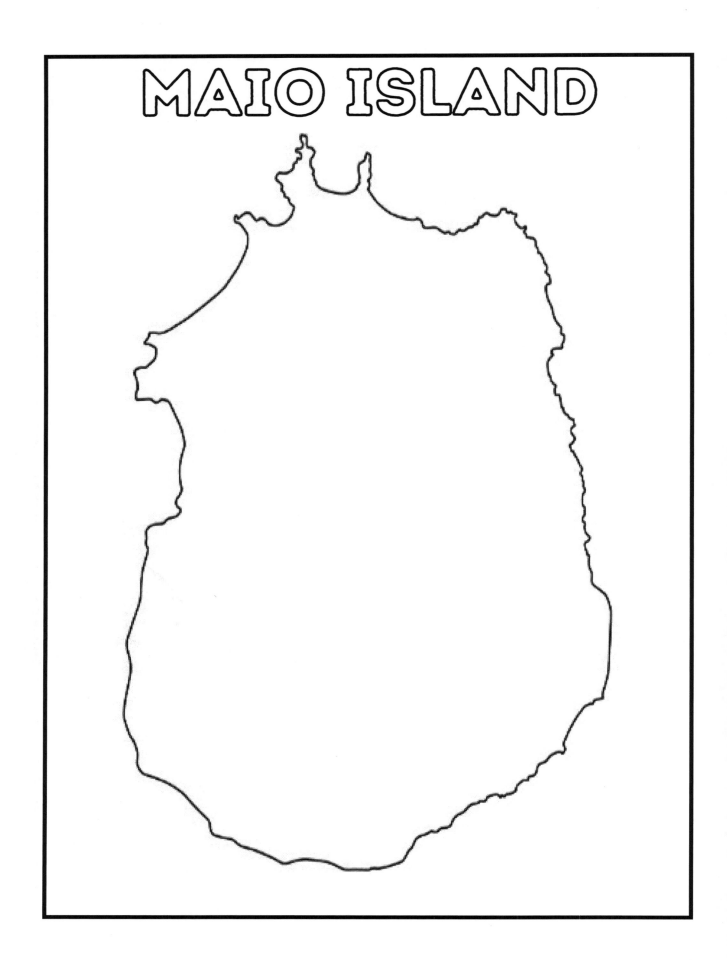

MAIO ISLAND

Maio is one of the islands that make up the archipelago of Cape Verde, located off the coast of West Africa. It is known for its beautiful beaches, peaceful atmosphere, and traditional Cape Verdean culture.

The island of Maio was first discovered by the Portuguese in the 15th century, during the Age of Exploration. It was initially used as a stopover point for ships traveling between Europe and Africa. Over time, the island became a center for agriculture, particularly for the production of salt, which was a valuable commodity in the region.

The major municipalities on the island of Maio are Vila do Maio, which is the capital and largest city, and Morro. Vila do Maio is the main hub of activity on the island, with a bustling market, shops, and restaurants. Morro is a smaller town known for its fishing industry and laid-back atmosphere.

Maio became a part of Cape Verde in the 15th century when the Portuguese colonized the archipelago. The island was used as a base for the slave trade and later became a center for agriculture and salt production. Today, Maio is a popular destination for tourists looking to experience the natural beauty and traditional culture of Cape Verde.

SAL ISLAND

SAL ISLAND

Sal is one of the ten islands that make up the Cape Verde archipelago, located off the coast of West Africa. It is known for its beautiful white sandy beaches and crystal-clear waters, making it a popular tourist destination.

The island of Sal was uninhabited when the Portuguese first arrived in the 15th century. It was used as a base for salt mining, hence the name "Sal," which means salt in Portuguese. The island's economy was largely based on salt production for many years.

The major municipalities on the island of Sal are Santa Maria, Espargos, and Palmeira. Santa Maria is the main tourist town on the island, known for its stunning beaches and vibrant nightlife. Espargos is the capital of Sal and serves as the main administrative center. Palmeira is a fishing village located on the west coast of the island.

Sal became a part of Cape Verde when the islands gained independence from Portugal in 1975. Since then, the island has seen significant development in the tourism sector, with many hotels, resorts, and restaurants catering to visitors from around the world.

Today, Sal is a popular destination for tourists looking to relax on the beach, enjoy water sports, and explore the island's natural beauty. With its warm climate, friendly locals, and stunning scenery, Sal continues to attract visitors seeking a tropical paradise.

SANTA LUZIA

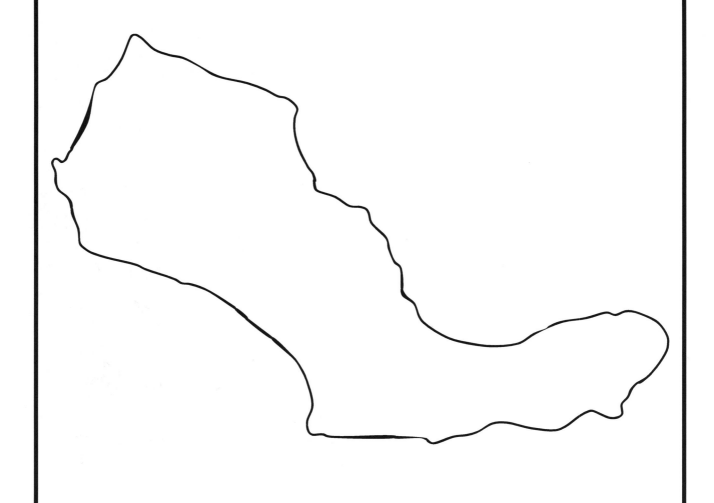

SANTA LUZIA

Santa Luzia is a small uninhabited island located in the Barlavento archipelago of Cape Verde. The island is part of the Barlavento group of islands, which also includes Santo Antão, São Vicente, São Nicolau, Sal, and Boa Vista.

Santa Luzia was discovered by Portuguese explorers in the 15th century during the Age of Discovery. The island was originally used as a grazing ground for goats and sheep, but due to its arid climate and lack of freshwater sources, it was never permanently settled by humans.

In the 19th century, Santa Luzia became a part of Cape Verde, which was a Portuguese colony at the time. The island was used as a penal colony for political prisoners and as a quarantine station for sailors with infectious diseases.

Today, Santa Luzia is a protected natural reserve and is known for its rugged coastline, pristine beaches, and unique flora and fauna. The island is a popular destination for eco-tourists and nature enthusiasts who come to explore its untouched landscapes and diverse wildlife.

There are no major municipalities on Santa Luzia, as the island is uninhabited. However, the nearby island of São Vicente serves as the administrative center for Santa Luzia and the other islands in the Barlavento group.

Overall, Santa Luzia's history is closely tied to the colonization of Cape Verde and its role as a natural reserve in the present day. The island's remote location and pristine environment make it a unique and special place in Cape Verde.

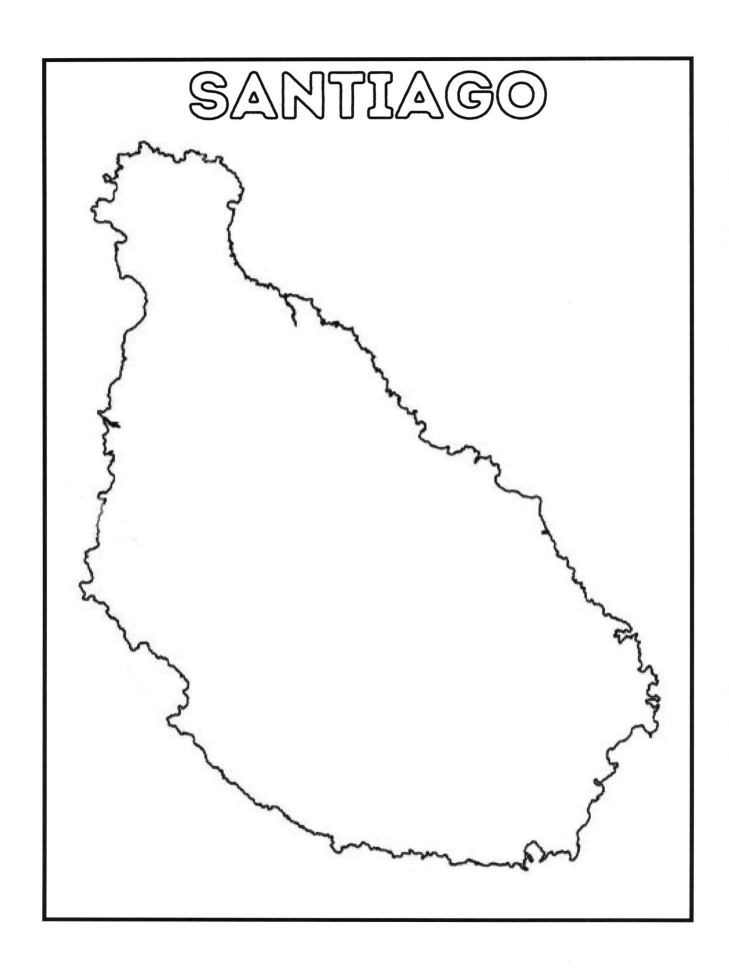

SANTIAGO

SANTIAGO

Santiago is the largest and most populous island in Cape Verde, located in the central part of the archipelago. It is home to the capital city of Praia, which is also the largest city in the country. Santiago has a rich history that dates back to the 15th century when it was first discovered by Portuguese explorers.

The island of Santiago has several major municipalities, including Praia, which is the capital city and the economic and political center of Cape Verde. Other important municipalities on the island include Santa Catarina, Santa Cruz, and Tarrafal.

Santiago played a significant role in the history of Cape Verde, particularly during the colonial period. The island was an important hub for the transatlantic slave trade, with many enslaved Africans passing through its ports on their way to the Americas. Santiago also served as a major agricultural center, producing crops such as sugar, coffee, and bananas.

In 1951, Cape Verde became an overseas province of Portugal, and Santiago continued to be an important center of economic and political activity. However, in the 1960s, the African Party for the Independence of Guinea and Cape Verde (PAIGC) began a guerrilla war against Portuguese colonial rule. The struggle for independence lasted until 1975 when Cape Verde gained its independence from Portugal.

After gaining independence, Santiago and the other islands of Cape Verde formed a new republic, with Praia as its capital. Santiago remains an important economic and cultural center in Cape Verde, with a diverse population and a vibrant arts and music scene. Today, the island is a popular tourist destination, known for its beautiful beaches, historic sites, and vibrant culture.

SANTO ANTÃO

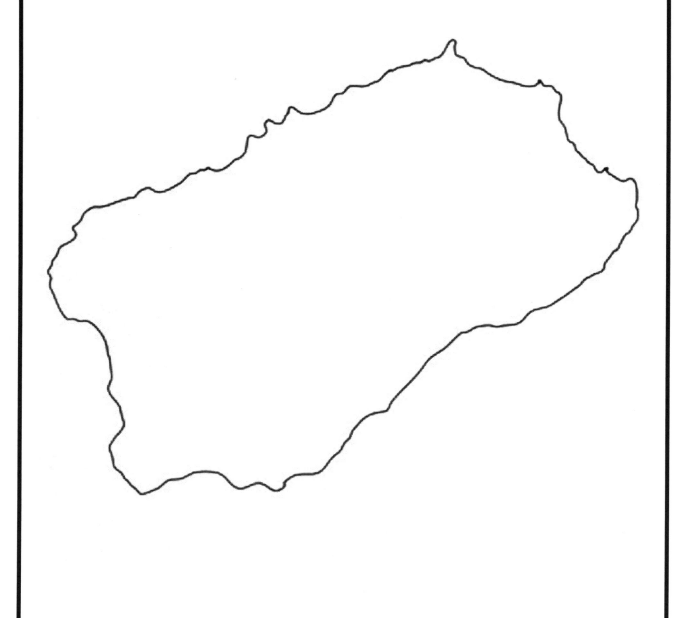

SANTO ANTÃO

Santo Antão is one of the ten islands that make up the Cape Verde archipelago in the Atlantic Ocean. It is the second largest island in Cape Verde and is known for its rugged terrain, lush valleys, and stunning coastline.

The island of Santo Antão was first inhabited by the Portuguese in the 15th century, shortly after they discovered the Cape Verde islands. The island's economy was initially based on agriculture, particularly the cultivation of sugarcane and cotton.

The major municipalities on Santo Antão include Porto Novo, Ribeira Grande, and Paul. Porto Novo is the largest municipality on the island and is home to the island's main port. Ribeira Grande is the oldest settlement on the island and was once the capital of Cape Verde. Paul is known for its picturesque valleys and hiking trails.

Santo Antão became a part of Cape Verde when the islands gained independence from Portugal in 1975. Since then, the island has experienced significant development and growth in tourism, particularly for its natural beauty and outdoor activities.

Today, Santo Antão is a popular destination for hikers, nature lovers, and adventure seekers looking to explore its rugged landscapes and experience the unique culture of Cape Verde.

SÃO NICOLAU

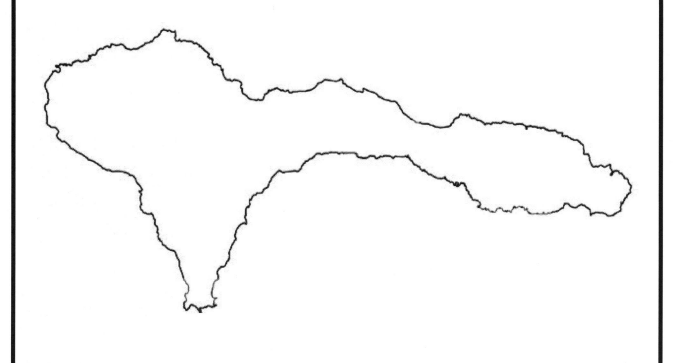

SÃO NICOLAU

São Nicolau is one of the ten islands that make up the Cape Verde archipelago in the Atlantic Ocean. The island has a rich history dating back to the 15th century when it was first discovered by Portuguese explorers.

The island was originally uninhabited, but over time, settlers from Portugal and other European countries began to establish communities on the island. São Nicolau became an important trading post in the region, with its natural harbors attracting merchants from around the world.

The major municipalities on the island include Ribeira Brava, Tarrafal de São Nicolau, and São Nicolau. Ribeira Brava is the largest town on the island and serves as the administrative center. Tarrafal de São Nicolau is known for its beautiful beaches and is a popular tourist destination.

São Nicolau officially became a part of Cape Verde in the 15th century when the Portuguese established a colony on the island. Over the centuries, the island has played an important role in the history of Cape Verde, serving as a key trading hub and a center of cultural exchange.

Today, São Nicolau is known for its stunning natural beauty, with rugged mountains, lush valleys, and pristine beaches. The island is also home to a vibrant cultural scene, with traditional music and dance festivals held throughout the year.

SÃO VICENTE

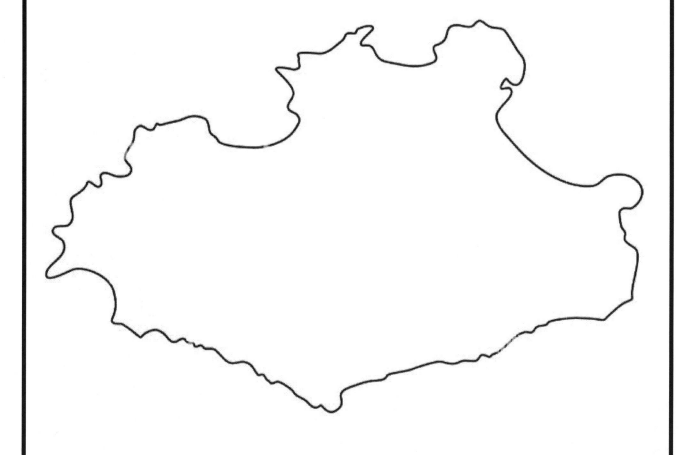

SÃO VICENTE

The island of São Vicente is one of the ten islands that make up the archipelago of Cape Verde, located off the coast of West Africa. The island was uninhabited when Portuguese explorers first arrived in the 15th century, and it was later settled by Portuguese colonists in the 16th century.

The main city on the island is Mindelo, which is also the second largest city in Cape Verde. Mindelo is known for its vibrant cultural scene, with a rich history of music, art, and literature. The city is also home to the country's largest port, making it an important hub for trade and commerce.

Other major municipalities on the island include São Pedro, which is known for its beautiful beaches and fishing villages, and Calhau, a small town on the eastern coast of the island.

São Vicente became a part of Cape Verde when the archipelago gained independence from Portugal in 1975. Since then, the island has developed into a popular tourist destination, known for its stunning beaches, lively music scene, and welcoming locals.

Overall, São Vicente has played an important role in the history and culture of Cape Verde, and continues to be a vibrant and dynamic part of the country.

<u>HISTORICAL DATES</u>

1. 1462 – Portuguese explorers discover and colonize the uninhabited islands of Cape Verde.

2. 1585 – Cape Verde becomes a major hub for the transatlantic slave trade.

3. 1951 – Cape Verde becomes an overseas province of Portugal.

4. 1975 – Cape Verde gains independence from Portugal.

5. 1991 – Multi-party democracy is established in Cape Verde.

6. 2005 – Cape Verde becomes a member of the World Trade Organization.

7. 2020 – The COVID-19 pandemic reaches Cape Verde, leading to widespread lockdowns and travel restrictions.

8. 2024 – Cape Verde celebrates its 50th anniversary of independence.

52775684R00020